Building materials

Since the beginning of time, people have constructed buildings for a variety of purposes. Depending on where they lived, they made their buildings with the natural materials that were locally available. Throughout the world, almost every material, whether animal, plant or mineral, has been used for building. Over the last century, the discovery of new man-made materials, together with great improvements in transport, have given modern builders a much greater choice of materials than ever before.

This book looks at the production of different building materials, and shows how they are used in different parts of the world. A freelance author for the last ten years, Graham Rickard has a special interest in building construction. He has written many educational books for children.

Focus on
BUILDING MATERIALS

Graham Rickard

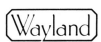

Focus on Resources series

Alternative Energy	Nuclear Fuel
Aluminium	Oil
Building Materials	Paper
Coal	Plastics
Cocoa	Radioactivity
Coffee	Rice
Copper	Rubber
Cotton	Salt
Dairy Produce	Seafood
Diamonds	Silk
Electricity	Silver
Fruit	Soya
Gas	Sugar
Glass	Tea
Gold	Timber
Grain	Vegetables
Iron and Steel	Water
Meat	Wool

First published in 1989 by
Wayland (Publishers) Ltd
61 Western Road, Hove
East Sussex, BN3 1JD, England

© Copyright 1989 Wayland (Publishers) Ltd

Editor: Susannah Foreman

Phototypeset by Kalligraphics Ltd, Horley, Surrey
Printed in Italy by G. Canale & C.S.p.A., Turin
Bound in the UK by The Bath Press, Avon

Frontispiece *The Golden Pavilion, Kyoto, Japan*

British Library Cataloguing in Publication Data

Rickard, Graham.
    Focus on building materials.
    1. Building materials
    I. Title   II. Series.
    691

    ISBN 1–85210–431–7

Contents

1. Building through the ages

People have always needed homes, to provide shelter from the weather and wild animals, to eat and sleep in and to store their possessions in safety. To build their homes, people have from the earliest times used whatever natural materials were locally available, such as rocks, trees or animal skins.

As society progressed, humankind started to construct many other types of buildings, in which they could work, keep their animals and pray to their gods. To help them to move from place to place, they built roads and bridges. In our modern society, we have many types of buildings for different uses, such as shops,

The mysterious structure of Stonehenge has stood for thousands of years, yet no one is sure why it was built.

offices, schools and sports centres.

The type of home that people live in depends on many factors, such as the climate, the inhabitants' way of life, and their choice of building material. Nomadic tribes, for example, tend to live in small, lightweight structures, which are quick to erect and easy to transport.

Until fairly recently, all building materials had to be obtained locally, and each area had its own quarry, brickworks or metal foundry to supply builders with all their needs. Improvements in transport gradually made it possible

The town of Sassi in southern Italy is built into the hillside, with the roofs of the houses forming the streets above them.

An English suburban house, built using modern materials and building techniques.

for builders to use materials from all over the world, such as asbestos from Canada and hardwoods from tropical forests.

Many new man-made materials, including plastics and reinforced concrete, have been discovered during this century and have given architects and builders a greater choice of materials and construction techniques than ever before. The type of material used in any modern building now depends not on what is locally available, but on other factors, such as cost, ease of use, and local building regulations.

7

2. Stone

Stone is one of the most durable and attractive of all building materials. Wherever there is a local supply, it has always been used to construct solid and long-lasting buildings. Many of the world's most impressive ancient monuments, such as England's Stonehenge, the pyramids of Egypt and the Indian Taj Mahal are built of stone, and will still be admired in future centuries.

The magnificent pyramids of Egypt were built from large blocks of stone.

Almost every size and shape of stone, from enormous blocks to very fine dust, can be used to make buildings. There are two main types of building stone. Ashlar is cut and shaped into regular blocks, and can be used to build entire structures, or to reinforce corners and door and

8

A grey stone castle built into a mountainside in 1570 in Yugoslavia.

It takes great skill to build a wall without using mortar in the joints. This 'dry stone' wall is in Japan.

window surrounds. Rubble buildings are made of rough natural lumps of stone, which may be laid in layers, called courses, or simply piled on top of each other. Both ashlar and rubble walls are usually held together with some kind of mortar, although skilled stonemasons can cut and lay the stones so accurately that there is no need for mortar and it is impossible to insert a penknife blade between them.

There are many different kinds of stone and they all have their different uses. Granite, for example, is very hard and makes strong, solid buildings, but sandstone and limestone are much easier to cut and work. Marble is a very beautiful stone, which is often used to make decorative floors and staircases, while slate splits easily into thin sheets, which are used for roofing. Flints can be split, or 'knapped', to reveal their dark, shiny interior. Even pebbles can be used to reinforce concrete, or to give an attractive 'pebble-dash' finish, by flinging them against wet cement on a wall.

Stone is relatively difficult to quarry and work with, and is expensive to handle and transport because it is so heavy. The high cost of stone means that it is not used as often as it was in the past, although there is a continual demand for stone to renovate old buildings. Some builders compromise, by using moulded concrete blocks, which include a high percentage of stone dust to make them more attractive.

3. Timber

An elephant moving timber in the vast forests of Thailand.

Forests cover one-third of the world's land surface. Wood is the oldest, most versatile, and easiest to use of all building materials. It is light, strong, easy to cut and shape with simple tools, and can be joined with glue, ropes, nails, screws or modern metal fasteners. It has good insulation properties and an attractive natural grained surface, which can be smoothed flat to take a coating of paint, varnish or other decorative finish. Wood is also very long-lasting if it is properly cared for and protected from damp.

Wood for building is called timber, and can be used to make floors, walls and roofs. All timber is divided into two types. Hardwoods, such as oak, teak and mahogany, are obtained from the slow-growing deciduous trees of tropical and temperate countries. These hardwoods are usually heavier and longer-lasting, and are used for the exposed outer parts of a building. The cheaper softwoods are produced from coniferous trees, such as pine, larch and spruce. Softwoods have less fibres than hardwoods and are easier to work.

The simplest way to build with timber is to lay whole tree trunks or branches on top of each other – the technique once used to build the traditional log cabins of Scandinavia and North America. But this method wastes a lot of timber, and nowadays trees are usually sawn into planks and sections of different thick-

thin veneer on each side, and is widely used in the construction industry. Paper is another important wood product, and is still sometimes used to make traditional Japanese houses.

Left *A wood turner in Thailand uses a lathe and chisel to shape the wood.*

Below *Repairing a traditional Australian timber house.*

nesses. This is an economical way of providing the maximum amount of usable timber from each tree. To prevent the timber from warping, it has to be 'seasoned', by storing it in a dry place until most of its natural moisture has evaporated.

Traditional timber houses, with weatherboard cladding, are still very popular in Australia, the USA and Scandinavia, where there is still a plentiful supply of timber. In modern Scandinavian and German factories, tree trunks enter at one end, and semi-assembled houses emerge at the other.

Wood by-products such as shavings, chips, sawdust and small blocks can be glued together and pressed into large sheets of chipboard, fibreboard and other wood products. Plywood is a strong and attractive material, covered with a

4. Earth, mud and clay

Even in areas with a shortage of stone and timber, there is usually a plentiful supply of soil. In many countries, earth and clay are a popular material for building walls and floors. When left unprotected, earth is soon washed away by heavy rain, or eroded by frost, so it is most suitable for building in hot, dry climates.

In Africa, mud homes are made by mixing soil with water, and shaping the mud by hand to make the walls. Small doors and windows are cut while the mud is still damp, and the thatched roof is added when the walls have dried and hardened in the sun.

In some Arab countries, builders use mud bricks to make thick walls, with tiny windows to keep out the sun's rays from the cool interior. In Mexico clay blocks are dried in the sun, before being used to build 'adobe' walls. A mixture of liquid clay is used to stick the adobe blocks together, and to give a smooth surface on each side of the wall.

Mud and clay can be made stronger by reinforcing it with some other material, such as

Thatched mud homes built at Wadi Rima, in the Yemen.

This cemetery in Egypt was made from bricks of dried mud.

mixture of soil and a small quantity of cement (or lime) is compacted into moulds, using a simple and inexpensive hand press, to produce strong and uniform soil blocks. Six people can produce 40 blocks an hour using this press, and the blocks can then be used in the same way as bricks. The new blocks last up to thirty years, and have already been used to build new villages in Kenya, Nigeria and the Caribbean.

In very cold countries, snow and ice are also used as construction materials. The Inuit, for example, build their temporary dome-shaped igloos from blocks of compacted snow.

Mud bricks are often used to make 'adobe' homes in Mexico.

straw, animal hair or cow dung. In some parts of Europe, such as south-west England, traditional cob walls are built from a mixture of clay, pebbles, sand and straw. To prevent the walls from collapsing under their own weight, each layer is left to dry before the next is added. The doors and windows are cut out with a sharp spade, and the walls are given a final waterproof coating of tar or limewash.

In developing countries, modern materials such as concrete and bricks have to be imported and are often too expensive to use. A new technique has been invented which may help to solve these countries' housing needs. A

5. Plant materials

Trees provide not only timber from their trunks, but also branches, twigs, leaves and bark, all of which can be used for building.

Wattle walls are made by weaving twigs around upright poles set in the ground, and are widely used to build houses in Thailand and parts of Africa. To make the walls more weatherproof, the wattle can be covered in a mixture of mud and cow dung – a construction technique known as 'wattle and daub'.

Many other plants, such as grasses, reeds, moss and heather, are all used for building, wherever there is a constant supply. In Africa, some people build simple 'Kirdi' shelters, which have a roof of grass on wooden poles to protect them from the fierce heat of the sun.

African dome-shaped 'beehive' huts are made from woven grass, with a wickerwork door.

In Ireland and Scandinavia, special spades are used to cut long strips of turf, which are sewn together with grass to make a living roof that is both warm and waterproof.

In the marshlands of southern Iraq, some reeds grow up to 7 m long. These are cut into long bundles, which are then lashed together at the top and set in the ground in rows. The line of tall arches is then joined together with horizontal poles, and covered with reed matting, to make a spectacular arched, green home.

Reed houses built on an island in Lake Titicaca in Peru.

Below *This diagram shows how 'wattle and daub' walls are constructed.*

Above *The roofs of these houses in Kashmir are made of living turf.*

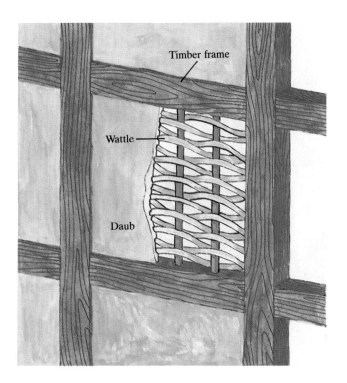

Timber frame

Wattle

Daub

Cotton is one of the world's most important plant materials, and has several uses in the building industry. Loosely woven into a material called 'scrim', it is used to reinforce plasterwork on interior corners. It can also be woven into heavier fabrics, such as duck and canvas, which are widely used to make tents and large marquees. Other plant fibres, such as jute and hemp, also have their uses – to make ropes and as a backing for bitumen-covered damp-proofing materials.

Plant materials are probably most useful for making thatched roofs. These are made from bundles of reeds or straw, attached with split twigs to a wooden frame. To shed rainwater efficiently, a thatched roof must have a fairly steep pitch, but a well-laid thatched roof is both warm and waterproof, and may last up to a hundred years.

6. Animal materials

Herds of animals, whether wild or domesticated, have always been a source of building materials. The skins of large animals are useful for covering a wooden framework, but almost every part of the animal can be used in some way. Thin strips of horn, for example, were once used to make windows, and even bones and hooves can be made into glue. Animal hair can also be used to reinforce other materials, such as mud and clay.

Lightweight homes made of animal materials are especially popular with nomadic people in various parts of the world. Nomadic people often live in barren regions, and wander from place to place in search of food and water for themselves and their herds of sheep and goats. The traditional tents of the North American Indians, called teepees, are made from a conical framework of long wooden poles, covered with animal skins that are stitched together.

Other nomadic people shear the fleeces from their flocks, and spin and weave the wool into fabric. The wandering Arab people, called the Bedouin, who live in the desert, make their low black tents from fabric woven from goat or camel hair. The Bedouin women weave long strips of the cloth, which are then sewn

Left *The black tents of the Bedouin are made from fabric woven from goat or camel hair.*

together and draped over a framework of poles. These are held in place by cords attached to wooden pegs in the ground. These tents are comfortable and easy to erect, pack up and carry when the Bedouin move on in search of new pastures.

In the colder climate of Mongolia and northern Iran, some nomads live in portable circular homes called 'yurts'. The yurt's light-weight wooden lattice frame is unfolded and covered with sheets of felt. This is made by pressing animal hairs together into a thick matting, rather than weaving them into fine material.

A yurt is made of a wooden frame covered with felt. The felt is made from animal hair pressed into thick matting.

7. Bricks

Bricks are regular-shaped blocks of clay, which are left to dry and then fired in a kiln at temperatures of around 900°C. When fired, the minerals in the clay fuse around the clay particles, to form a strong, hard material, which can be used in much the same way as stone.

Hand-made bricks of different shapes and sizes have been in use for thousands of years, but in many countries they are now produced by automatic extrusion machines, which squeeze out the clay in long strips, and slice them to the right size with wire cutters. The standard size of brick is 225×112×75 mm.

This fits comfortably in an adult human hand, but different sizes of brick are also made for special uses.

There are many different grades of brick. 'Commons' are used for internal walls, facing bricks for external surfaces, and extra-strong engineering bricks are used to lay the underground foundations and footings of a building. Perforated bricks have holes in them, to save weight or to provide ventilation.

The Chan-chan ruins on the north coast of Peru show the use of handmade bricks.

Most bricks are porous and can absorb several times their own weight of water, so a bitumen damp-proof course (DPC) is usually laid above ground level in brick walls, to prevent damp from rising up the wall. Outer brick walls are usually built as two separate skins, with an air cavity in the middle to provide ventilation, insulation and an effective barrier against driving rain.

It is easier to build with brick than with stone, but the techniques are very similar. The bricks are laid in horizontal courses, with the vertical joints overlapping to prevent weaknesses in the wall. Bricklayers use mortar to bond the bricks together. Bricks laid lengthways are called 'stretchers', and those laid end-on are 'headers'. Some bricks have a cavity, called a 'frog', on one side, to hold the mortar. Bricks are easily split with a sharp blow from a trowel. Bricklayers use a spirit level and a plumbline to check that the courses are even and the wall is vertical.

Double-skinned walls, made of brick and concrete blocks, are often used in modern houses.

8. Cement and concrete

Stone and brick both need some form of binding material, called mortar, to hold them together. At one time, almost all mortar consisted of a mixture of sand, water and lime; the lime (calcium oxide) was produced by heating limestone (calcium carbonate) in a kiln. In 1824, a British stonemason, Joseph Aspdin, invented Portland cement, which has replaced lime as a masonry binding agent, and is now manufactured in huge quantities all over the world. Cement is a powdered mixture of calcium silicates and aluminates which, when mixed with water, undergoes complicated processes and sets into a hard, solid mass.

A type of concrete was used by the Romans over 2,000 years ago. Modern concrete came into use only after the invention of Portland cement. Concrete consists of a mixture of cement, water and anaggregate of sand, gravel and broken stones. Concrete sets very hard, and increases in strength over many decades, making it an ideal structural material. Concrete can be given even greater tensile strength by reinforcing it with metal bars (up to 50 mm in diameter), a technique invented in France in 1850. If the metal bars are stretched and kept under tension while the concrete sets, they produce pre-stressed concrete, which is even stronger than reinforced concrete, and will not bend even under heavy loads.

While the outer walls of this house are brick, the inner walls are made of concrete blocks. These are quicker to build with than bricks.

Concrete is widely used to make exciting modern buildings, and can be cast into almost any shape. As well as its great strength, concrete has very good fire-proofing qualities, making it an ideal material for building skyscrapers and tall office blocks. It can be poured wet from a concrete-mixer lorry, and moulded on site in wood or metal shuttering, or pre-cast in sections in a factory, for assembly on site. Concrete can also be sprayed into shape over a metal-mesh shell. Sand-blasting gives an attractive finish by revealing the pebbles beneath the smooth concrete surface.

Concrete can also be made into building blocks, which are much larger than bricks, and quicker to build with. Lightweight blocks, with good sound and heat insulation, are made by bubbling air through the concrete, before it sets in moulds. Ash and volcanic rock are sometimes mixed into the concrete, to make the blocks cheaper to produce.

Reinforced concrete can be used to make large elegant structures, such as this elevated road.

9. Glass

Glass has been used as a decorative material since about 4000 BC. Beautiful coloured glass windows have been used for centuries in churches and mosques. However, it is only in the last century that glass has been cheap enough to use on a large scale as a building material. It is very difficult to make flat, clear glass, and it was not until 1959 that the English company Pilkington discovered the process of floating molten glass on a bath of molten tin, to produce large quantities of cheap, flat glass.

Glass is a man-made material. Most glass is made by heating a mixture of sand (silica), soda (sodium carbonate) and lime (calcium carbonate), to a temperature of over 1500°C. However, by altering the ingredients of this basic 're-cipe', the properties of glass can be drastically changed and tailored to suit a variety of different uses, such as car windscreens or radiation-proof inspection windows, for use in nuclear power stations.

Glass is used to great effect in modern buildings, such as Les Halles in Paris.

Without glass, our buildings would be dark and gloomy places. Glass is used not only for windows, but also as large cladding panels to form the outer 'skin' of modern buildings. Modern types of solar control glass reflect or absorb the heat from the sun's rays, while still allowing light to pass through.

Although glass lets in light, it also lets out valuable heat in the winter. Double glazed panels have two layers of glass with a layer of air in the middle, and have good thermal and sound insulation. Glass is naturally a very fragile material, but it can be made stronger in several different ways — by laminating it with layers of wire mesh, for example. Some modern types of toughened glass are even bulletproof, and are widely used in offices and shops.

A magnificent stained glass window in Chester Cathedral, in England.

This glass skyscraper reflects the architecture in Dallas, Texas.

Glass can be spun into fine fibres, and made into a matting which is widely used as an insulating material, and to reinforce concrete and various plastics. Glass fibres are also totally flameproof, and can be woven into fabric, to make stage curtains for cinemas, theatres and other public places.

This versatile material can also be moulded into lightweight hollow bricks, which can be used in the same way as ordinary bricks, to create attractive interior walls and partitions. In the USA, entire houses have been made from empty bottles!

23

10. Steel

Steel is a very strong, lightweight material, used to build slender and graceful structures, such as bridges, over very long spans. Steel is a type of iron that contains between 0.1 and 1.5 per cent carbon, and was first discovered in 1856. It is made by heating iron ore in a blast furnace to produce pig iron, which is added to melted-down scrap iron before being further purified in an open hearth or electric-arc furnace.

Its properties can be varied enormously by heat treatment, or by the addition of other metals, such as chromium, manganese and vanadium, to make different steel alloys.

Steel is widely used in almost every modern industry, and it plays a very important part in the world's economy; over 400,000 tonnes of steel are produced every week in the UK alone.

In the construction industry, most steel is in the form of 'I'- or 'H'-shaped reinforced steel joists (RSJs) and girders. These are used to make sky-scrapers and tower blocks of offices and flats. The girders are lifted into place with large cranes, and each storey is built up in a series of box shapes to form the framework or 'skeleton' of the building. Sometimes the crane tower is left inside the completed building to be used as a lift shaft.

Steel girders can be cut to size with grindwheels or oxyacetylene torches, and they are easily joined together with bolts and rivets, or by welding. When the framework is complete, it is strong enough to support the whole weight of the building, and the outer walls can be filled in with cladding panels of almost any material. RSJs are also built into many houses to support the weight of the walls over doorways, chimneys and window openings. These are known as lintels.

Steel can also be woven into strong, thick cables, which are often used to support large-span suspension bridges. Many nails, screws and other fixings are made of some form of steel, and steel rods and mesh are used to reinforce concrete.

Left *A crane lifts a floor section into position on a steel skyscraper in New York.*

Because of its strength and light weight, steel is used to build bridges, such as this railway bridge in Japan.

11. Building around the world

Building a Yurt

A wooden trellis is built to form a circular fence.

A sturdy pole is set in the centre to hold the roof supports.

Felt, made from matted sheeps' wool is stretched over the framework.

The Yurt can be assembled in half an hour.

Building an Igloo

Snow blocks are set in a ring and their top surfaces are sloped.

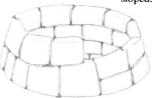

More blocks are laid on top, with each layer leaning inwards.

The dome is completed with one block to fill the hole in the top.

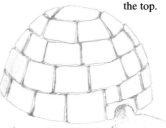

A snow tunnel lets in people but traps cold air.

26

Building a Reed House

1. Large reeds up to 7m long are cut and tied together in bundles.

2. The ends of each bundle are set into holes in the ground.

3. They are curved to make the shape of the house.

4. Mats are woven from reeds to make the walls and roof.

5. The walls can be rolled back in summer to let in cool breezes, while in winter the thick walls keep out the cold wind.

12. Other metals

Civilization took a great step forward when people first learnt how to mine and smelt ore to make different metals, such as iron and bronze. Metals have always been used to make many different parts of buildings, such as water pipes, hinges and nails.

But it was not until the Industrial Revolution of the eighteenth century that metals started to be used as a structural material. In 1779 the world's first cast-iron bridge was erected in England, at Coalbrookdale in Shropshire. This was seen as a great engineering achievement, and iron was quickly accepted as a building material that could be used to construct buildings and ships, as well as bridges.

When steel was found to be a much stronger metal, it soon took over from iron as a structural material. Iron is still used, however, to make nails, guttering and drain covers.

Copper is easily worked and is a very good conductor of heat and electricity, which makes it a useful metal in the construction industry.

The world's first iron bridge, at Coalbrookdale in England, caused a sensation when it was built.

The houses in this shanty town in Brunei are made of sheets of corrugated iron.

It is used mainly to make water pipes, hot water tanks and electrical cables, but it can also be combined with other metals to make useful alloys, such as bronze and brass. Brass is an attractive metal that does not rust, and can be made into screws, rivets and decorative items such as door handles and light switches.

After oxygen and silicone, aluminium is the third commonest element on the earth's surface. It is a light corrosion-free metal, which is fairly weak in its pure form, but can be strengthened by alloying it with copper, manganese or other metals. It is easy to work and is widely used to make door and window frames which need no maintenance. Aluminium is also a very good conductor of heat and electricity, and now replaces copper in some types of electrical cable.

Lead and zinc are both very soft metals, flat sheets of which are used to provide waterproof roof flashings around chimneys and other obstacles. Zinc is also widely used in paints, and as a coating to protect steel from rusting. Zinc-coated wire and bolts are commonly used, and galvanized corrugated roofing sheets are sometimes used as roofs, especially in poor 'shanty towns' which are often found on the outskirts of large cities.

13. Plastics

Modern kitchens often have vinyl floor coverings, which are attractive and easy to clean.

Plastics are synthetic materials that can be formed into usable products by heating, milling, moulding and other processes. In fact, the word 'plastic' is derived from the Greek *plastikos*, meaning 'to form'. Plastics are composed of giant molecules, called polymers, with very long chains of short molecules, held together by chemical bonds. Some polymers, such as rubber, occur naturally, but most plastics are based on synthetic resins and fibres. The first plastic, called Xylonite, was produced in England in 1862, but it was not until the 1920s that modern plastics began to appear. Today the plastics industry is a huge, worldwide business, and scientists are continually discovering new types of plastic.

Most plastics soften but do not melt when heated, and can easily be moulded into different shapes. Plastic is tough, light and cheap, and can be made transparent or given any colour with the use of dyes and pigments. Plastic has very good thermal and electrical resistance, and is such a versatile substance that it has largely replaced many more traditional materials, such as wood and rubber.

There are many different types of plastic, and each type is suitable for different uses. PVC (polyvinyl chloride) has a very good combination of stiffness and strength, and is used for drainpipes, guttering and cheap corrugated roofing sheets. Polyester resin can be reinforced with glass fibres to make a light and strong material, used to make boats, car bodies and cladding panels for buildings. Expanded polystyrene has very good sound and thermal insulation properties, and can either be made into sheets or injected into wall cavities. Polythene sheeting is widely used as vapour seals and damp-proof membranes, while silicone solutions can be applied to walls and ceilings to combat damp problems.

Vinyl floor-coverings are tough, waterproof and attractive. Modern architraves and skirting boards are often made of plastic, which is easy to clean and never needs painting. Plastics are also used to make paints and glues, while plastic fibres greatly increase the strength of concrete.

An exciting and quick way of building is to inflate a giant plastic balloon, which is then covered with a layer of fibreglass and plastic resin. When the resin has set, the balloon is deflated, and holes are cut in the dome-shaped structure for doors and windows.

Plastic water fittings are cheap and easy to use.

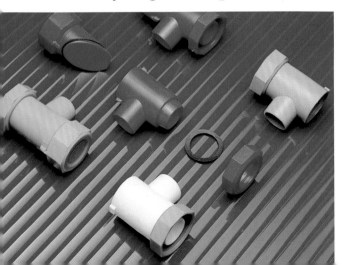

Guttering and drainpipes are now often made of plastic, which, unlike iron, never corrodes.

14. Asbestos

Asbestos is the name given to a group of minerals. The crystals of these minerals form long, strong fibres, which are flexible, fireproof and resistant to heat, electricity and chemical attack. These properties make asbestos a very useful material in many aspects of the construction industry. Although they all look much the same, the three main types of asbestos are known as white, blue and brown.

The main producers of asbestos are the USSR, Canada and Brazil. Asbestos-rich rock is mined and crushed, and the fibres are separated by blowing them away from the rock with jets of air. The longest fibres can be spun or woven, and used to insulate electrical cables in furnaces and nuclear reactors. Asbestos pipes and

An asbestos mine in Newfoundland, Canada.

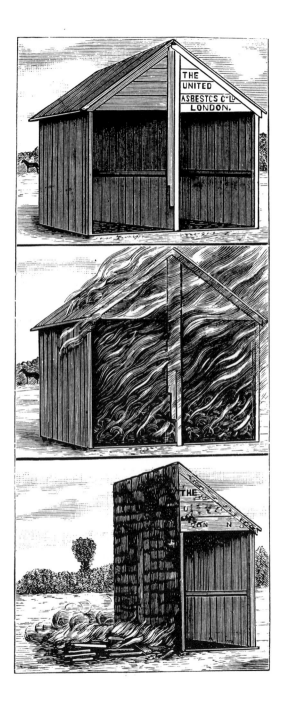

filters are widely used in chemical plants. Firemen and astronauts used to wear protective suits with a heat-proof asbestos filling.

The smaller fibres and asbestos dust are mixed with cement, and moulded into sheets and pipes for the building industry. Flat or corrugated asbestos sheets make a cheap covering for walls and roofs, and layers of asbestos are sometimes used in fireproof doors.

In the early 1970s, many people became concerned about the dangers of asbestos. Several countries have now recognized the health risks of using this material, and have banned its use. Asbestosis is an often-fatal lung disease caused by inhaling asbestos fibres; the air sacs in patients' lungs become thickened and scarred, and sufferers are likely to develop lung cancer. Asbestos dust is also a known cause of an industrial disease known as mesothelioma.

Even in countries that have banned its use, the removal and disposal of asbestos from derelict buildings remains a problem. Workmen have to wear protective clothing, helmets and breathing apparatus. The working area has to be sealed off and hosed down to prevent the escape of dust, and the asbestos material has to be carefully sealed in airtight bags before it can be safety disposed of. When bonded in cement, asbestos is less of a health risk, but care must still be taken when cutting this material.

Left *A nineteenth-century advertisement showing the fire-proofing qualities of asbestos. The right side of the hut has been treated with asbestos paint and survives the fire.*

15. Roofing materials

A sound and waterproof roof is perhaps the most important part of any structure, and the most difficult to build.

Most roofs have a timber framework, covered with a layer of cladding material. Flat roofs are popular in many hot, dry countries, but pitched roofs are much better at shedding water in wetter climates. The exact angle of pitch depends on the choice of material: clay tiles need a pitch of about 45°, modern cement tiles need only 17°, while thatch should be pitched at 75° to shed water effectively.

Flat or curved roof tiles are made from fired clay, in much the same way as bricks. Overlapping layers of tiles are hung on horizontal roof battens with wooden pegs, rustproof nails, or with 'nibs' – small projections on the underside of the tile. Specially shaped tiles are used to cover the ridges, hips and valleys on a roof, and tiles are usually laid over an inner waterproof skin of bituminous roofing felt. In some areas, slabs of stone, split slates, cement tiles or wooden shingles are used in the same way as clay tiles.

Sheets of soft metal, usually lead or zinc, are bent into shape to seal the joints where the tiles meet a chimney, dormer window or some other

Right *A thatcher sets to work, laying bundles of straw on the roof.*

obstacle. At one time lead was used to cover entire roofs, especially on churches and cathedrals, but it is now very expensive and needs skilful handling.

Bundles of plant material, such as reeds, straw or grass, can be attached to a wooden framework, to provide an effective thatched roof. Thatch can be a fire hazard, and often needs a covering of wire netting to keep out animals and birds.

Thatch is a very good form of natural insulation, but most other roofing materials allow heat to escape from buildings. In modern buildings, some form of roof insulation, such as glass-fibre matting, is laid in the loft space, to prevent heat loss, and cut down on fuel bills.

Curved pantiles are often used on the roofs of houses in mediterranean countries.

The Grand Palace at Bangkok in Thailand is roofed with brightly coloured glazed tiles.

35

16. Plaster

Many building materials, such as bricks and clay, are often rendered with a smooth coating, to make them waterproof, fireproof, or more attractive. Different sorts of plaster have been used for many centuries to render walls and ceilings, giving a smooth surface that will easily accept paint or wallpaper. Wealthy people's homes were once decorated with extremely ornate moulded plaster ceilings, some of which can still be seen in stately homes that are open to the public.

The traditional formula for making plaster is a mixture of lime, sand and water, which hardens when dry by a chemical reaction with carbon dioxide in the atmosphere. A hard plaster of clay and sand can also be used to give a decorative rendering, known as 'stucco'.

Modern plasters are based on gypsum, a white mineral often formed by the evaporation of seawater. Gypsum is hydrated calcium sulphate, which when heated loses water, and becomes plaster of Paris. On internal walls and ceilings, plaster was once applied over a layer of wooden laths. Today, large sheets of plasterboard – a layer of plaster sandwiched between two layers of paper – are nailed to battens, to give a much smoother base.

Left *Large sheets of plasterboard are nailed to the wall to give a smooth base for the plaster.*

Plaster is sold in the form of powder, which is mixed with water into a thick creamy paste. Rough walls of stone or brick are first given a rendering coat of cement and sand, before being covered with a smooth layer of plaster. A plasterer has to work fairly fast, and mixes only small amounts of plaster at a time, because it dries very quickly. With a board of wet plaster in one hand and a trowel in the other, the plasterer applies it as evenly as possible, before smoothing it off with a metal or plastic 'float'. On outer corners, the plaster is laid over an angled piece of metal beading, which reinforces the plaster and protects it from knocks. It is sometimes difficult to achieve a smooth join where walls meet the floor or ceiling, and these areas are often covered with an architrave or skirting board.

Below *Wet plaster is smoothed on to walls and ceilings with a large trowel.*

Left *Intricate gilded plaster mouldings at the Royal Pavilion in Brighton.*

17. Paints and preservatives

Many building materials need regular maintenance to prevent them from deteriorating. Iron and steel, for example, are both eaten away by corrosion, while timber can be attacked by insects and fungi, such as wet or dry rot. There are many types of protective coating that can be applied to building materials, including paints and varnishes, and there have been great advances in these treatments over the last few decades.

Paint was used as a decoration for thousands of years before it was ever used as a protective coating. The delicate wall paintings in the caves at Lascaux, in France, for example, date back as far as 15,000 BC. The first use of protective coatings was by the ancient Egyptians, who used pitch and balsam to seal the timbers of their ships. Exposed wood in buildings was not protected until the Middle Ages, when it was sometimes coated with a layer of hand-made paint, using egg-white and other expensive and secret ingredients. Most buildings still remained unpainted until the eighteenth century, when the use of linseed oil and zinc oxide produced a rapid expansion in the paint manufacturing industry.

Paint consists of coloured dyes and pigments, suspended in a fluid that sets into a tough film and binds the pigment to the painted surface. There are many different types of paint for

A layer of gloss paint will protect wooden windows and doors for several years.

Wood can also be protected by applying a waterproof coating of varnish.

different surfaces and applications, and they can be applied by brush, roller or spray. Primers are used to seal and protect both wood and metal, while water-based emulsion paints are used to decorate interior walls and ceilings. Gloss paints are oil-based and are usually applied on top of an undercoat, to give a protective shiny skin to wood and metals. Masonry paints, for covering external brick, stone or cement walls, often contain plastics. These set to a tough weatherproof finish, which should last for several years.

Varnishes and lacquers are liquid coating materials containing a resin that dries to a hard transparent film. They are usually clear, but sometimes contain pigments.

Timber is often treated before use by immersing it under pressure in a bath of chemicals that protect it from attack by insects or fungi. Tar-based wood treatments are widely available. A method recently developed uses rods of preservatives, which are inserted into the timber, and are gradually absorbed over a long period of time.

18. Ceramics

Ceramics are defined as materials that are made by heating non-metallic inorganic substances. Bricks, tiles and glass are all ceramic materials, but there are many others that are widely used in building construction throughout the world.

Baked clay is used to make several kinds of product. Refractory materials can withstand very high temperatures, and are used to line furnaces and kilns. Earthenware is hard, but is very porous unless it is glazed with a vitreous coating of fired silicate. Stoneware is made from clay that contains more silicates and is fired at a higher temperature. It is very strong, almost impervious to water, and has a semi-glazed finish. Both earthenware and stoneware can be moulded into drainage pipes and chimney pots.

Square, red quarry tiles are very hard-wearing, and are a popular flooring material in many countries. Thin flat tiles with a decorative glazed finish are both waterproof and attractive, and are often cemented around sinks and baths to protect the surrounding walls from damp. Small enamelled tiles, often brightly coloured, can be used to create beautiful mosaics on walls and floors.

Porcelain was first developed by Chinese potters about a thousand years ago. It is a fine white ceramic with a glass-like finish. To make porcelain, fine clay is mixed with other materials, including china clay (kaolin), and

fired at temperatures of up to 1400°C. Depending on the type of porcelain, the glaze may have to be applied afterwards and hardened in a second firing. Porcelain is totally impervious to water, and is a very hygienic material, with a smooth, hard surface that is very easy to clean. A form of porcelain is commonly used to make wash basins and toilets.

Making tiny mosaic tiles at Ravenna in northern Italy.

A beautiful ceramic fireplace, designed and made by Marian Brandiss, a well-known ceramicist.

Most ceramics are very resistant to electricity, and are often used to house high-power fuses and other electrical components. Small porous ceramic pipes are sometimes inserted into damp walls, to absorb the moisture and help it evaporate.

19. New materials

Today's builders have a greater choice of materials than every before, and yet more materials are constantly being discovered. Many materials that were originally developed for use in the aerospace industry are now being used for building. Teflon, for example, was first discovered by accident in the 1930s, but was not really developed until the 1960s 'space-race'. It is still the most slippery substance known to us, and is used as a lubricant coating in almost every modern industry, including building construction.

Carbon fibre is one of the most exciting modern materials. It is made by heating synthetic textile fibres to produce long silky threads of pure carbon. These threads are 8 times stronger than steel, and are used to reinforce resins, ceramics and metals to produce super-strong materials. It is still very expensive, and is usually made into aircraft and space rocket components, but carbon fibre could play a very important part in the construction industry of the future.

Space research has also produced ultra-thin light metal foils to reflect heat away from the surface of satellites and spacecraft. These foils are now used in several insulation materials.

Materials discovered in space research may soon become everyday building materials.

Titanium is a very strong metal, which is light, flexible, easy to work, and resistant to corrosion. Combining titanium with other metals has produced many new lightweight alloys, with very high strength/weight ratios, which could be very useful in future building.

The exploration of space is about to enter a new era, with the building of large permanent space stations. This new research programme will give rise to even more new materials, although at first they will have to be manufactured on earth and transported into space. In space itself, the conditions of zero-gravity and lack of atmosphere could make it possible to manufacture many new materials, such as perfect crystals and spherical formations, which are impossible to make on earth.

Structures in space can also be much more fragile and delicate than on earth, because they have far less weight to support. In the more distant future, astronauts could perhaps mine raw materials from planets and asteroids, and process them in space factories to manufacture their own buildings and spacecraft.

New materials and better techniques will make the homes of the future better places to live in.

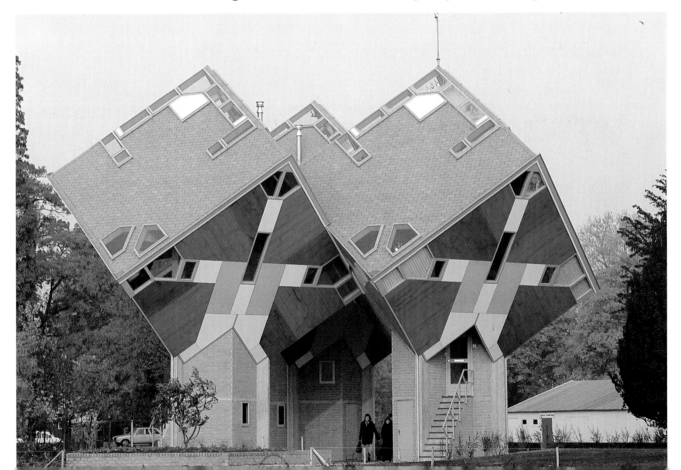

Facts and figures

Brick

65% used in houses.

35% used in commercial,
industrial and institutional buildings.

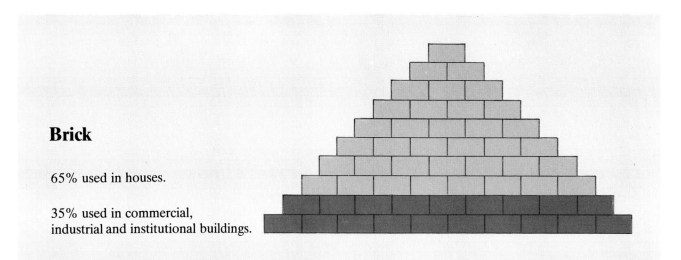

World Timber Production

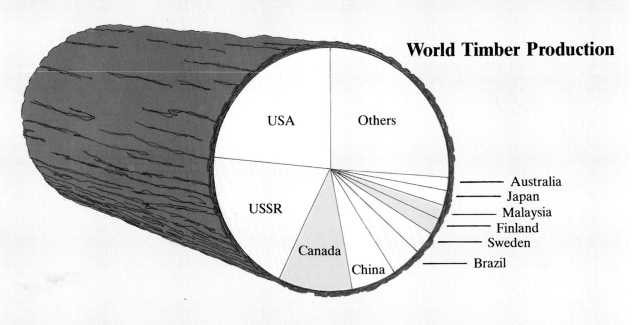

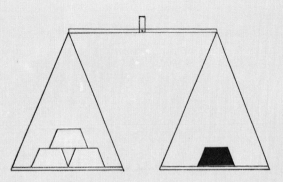

Aluminium weighs only one third as much as copper or steel.

Steel manufacture in the U.S.A.

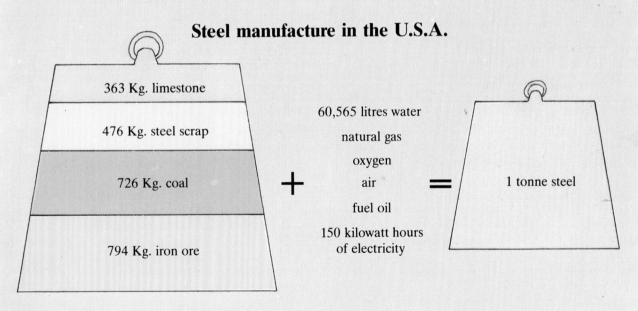

363 Kg. limestone

476 Kg. steel scrap

726 Kg. coal

794 Kg. iron ore

60,565 litres water

natural gas

oxygen

air

fuel oil

150 kilowatt hours
of electricity

+

=

1 tonne steel

Annual world production is about 700 million tonnes.

Glossary

Adobe Bricks of clay, which are dried in the sun.

Aggregate The sand and stones in concrete.

Alloy A combination of two or more metals, or a metal with some other substance.

Ashlar Building stone cut into regular smooth-faced blocks.

Balsam A resin obtained from trees.

Bitumen A black sticky substance obtained from tar.

Cast-iron A strong but brittle type of moulded iron, containing a large amount of carbon.

Cob A mixture of clay, straw and stones, used for building walls.

Coniferous Trees that carry cones and have evergreen leaves.

Course An even horizontal layer of stones or bricks in a wall.

Deciduous Trees with broad leaves, which are shed every year.

Dormer window A window that projects from a roof or attic space.

Flashing Strip of metal used to prevent a roof from leaking at the joins.

Footings The wide base of a wall below ground level.

Foundations The strong base of a building, usually made by filling trenches with concrete.

Foundry A place where metal is cast into moulds.

Galvanized Metal that is protected with a coating of zinc.

Hardwood Durable timber produced from deciduous trees.

Insulation Material that resists the transmission of heat, electricity or sound.

Joist A beam made of timber, reinforced concrete or wood.

Laminating Bonding together thin sheets of material.

Lath Thin strip of wood for supporting plaster.

Lattice A framework of thin strips of wood.

Lime A calcium compound obtained from limestone.

Limewash A mixture of lime and water for whitewashing walls.

Mineral Natural inorganic material that occurs in the surface of the earth.

Mortar A mixture of sand and water with cement (or lime), used to bond bricks or stonework.

Pitch 1) The angle of a sloping roof 2) A thick sticky black liquid obtained from tar.

Plumbline A weight on a string, used to check that a wall is vertical.

Plywood Thin sheets of timber glued together with the grain in alternate directions, for added strength.

Refractory Able to withstand high temperatures.

Render To apply a smooth coat of plaster, clay or cement to a wall.

Shuttering Wood or metal moulds for shaping concrete.

Silicone A synthetic material used as a lubricant and water-repellent.

Softwood Timber from coniferous trees.

Spirit level A straight bar of wood or metal, with an air bubble trapped in liquid, used to show if a wall is level.

Tensile The ability to withstand strain along a length of material.

Thermal To do with temperature.

Valley The point where two roof angles meet.

Veneer Very thin sheet of wood, applied to surfaces for decorative effect.

Vitreous Made of or resembling glass.

Wattle and daub A method of building walls, by covering woven twigs with a layer of mud or clay.

Weatherboard Horizontal planks of wood on the outside of a house.

Sources of further information

For more information on the subjects covered in this book, please contact the following organizations:

Building Research Advisory Service
Garston
Watford WD2 7JR

National House Building Council
58 Portland Place
London W1N 4BU

Cement and Concrete Association
Wexham Springs
Slough SL3 6PL

Timber Research and Development Association
Hughenden Valley
High Wycombe
Bucks

In New Zealand, please contact:

Building Research Association of N.Z.
290 Great South Road
Greenlane
Auckland

In Australia, please contact:

CSIRO Building Section
9 Queens Road
Melbourne
Victoria 3000

Sydney Building Information Service
525 Elizabeth Street
Sydney 2000

Books to read

CLARKE, D. *How It's Built* (Marshall Cavendish, 1979)
DAVEY, N. *The History of Building Materials* (Phoenix House)
GEE, A. *Looking at Houses* (Batsford, 1983)
GRUMMITT, N. *The Building Trades* (Wayland, 1973)
JONES, E. *Buildings and Building Sites* (Blandford, 1970)
KURTH, H. *Concrete* (World's Work, 1972)
KURTH, H. *Houses and Homes* (World's Work, 1980)
PENOYRE, J. & RYAN, M. *The Observer's Book of Architecture* (Frederick Warne, 1975)
RICKARD, G. *Building Homes* (Wayland, 1988)

Picture Acknowledgements

The author and publishers would like to thank the following for allowing their illustrations to be reproduced in this book: the Cement and Concrete Association 19,20; Chapel Studios *frontispiece* ,6, 7 (both), 8, 9 (both), 10, 11 (both), 12, 13 (both), 14, 15, 18, 21, 22, 23 (both), 24, 25, 29, 30, 31 (both), 34, 35 (both), 36, 37 (both), 38, 39, 40, 41, 42; Mary Evans Picture Library 28; the Hutchison Library 16, 17, 32; Ann Ronan Picture Library 33; Science Photo Library 42; ZEFA 43. The artwork on pages 15, 26–7 and 44–5 was supplied by Jenny Hughes.

Index